The Discovery Books are prepared

under the educational supervision of

Mary C. Austin, Ed.D.

Reading Specialist and

Professor of Education

Western Reserve University

A DISCOVERY BOOK

GARRARD PUBLISHING COMPANY
CHAMPAIGN, ILLINOIS

The Wright Brothers

Kings of the Air

by Mervyn D. Kaufman

illustrated by Gray Morrow

For Christopher Pinkham,

whose father, the Professor,

was always right.

Contents

The Wright Brothers: Kings of the Air

Chapter *1*

Toys That Flew

"Boys, your father is home!"

Wilbur and Orville heard their mother calling. In an instant the boys were running down the stairs.

Though Orville Wright was only seven, he could almost keep up with eleven-year-old Wilbur. Both of them ran so fast they almost knocked over their sister. Little Kate was four.

7

Their father was just coming in the door. He was a minister. A year before, in 1877, he had become a bishop. His work often kept him away from the Wright home in Cedar Rapids, Iowa.

"Well, how are my boys?" he asked.

"I'm fine, Father," said Wilbur.

"Me too," said Orville. "What's that in your pocket?"

"I can never hide anything from *you*," Bishop Wright said, chuckling. "It's a surprise." He turned his back. The boys saw him remove a package from his pocket and unwrap it.

Suddenly he turned around. "Here, catch this." He tossed a small object into the air. It sailed up to the ceiling on a pair of whirling wings.

"It flies!" cried Orville.

8

"It's like a bat," said Wilbur. After a moment the wings slowed down. The "bat" floated to the floor.

"It's a new toy," said Bishop Wright. "The inventor calls it a *helicopter*."

Wilbur picked up the helicopter. He and Orville saw that it was made of pieces of wood, rubber bands and cork. There was a paper wing at each end.

"You wind it by twisting the rubber bands," the Bishop said. "They make the wings spin around."

Wilbur and Orville took the new toy outdoors. They laughed and shouted as it flew. Their older brothers laughed too, when they came home from school.

"Look at those two," Lorin said to Reuchlin. "You'd think *they* had built that helicopter."

Later, when the toy was too worn to fly, Wilbur and Orville did build one themselves. They were careful to make it the same as the old one.

"Now let's make a *big* one," Orville said one day. "A big helicopter should fly higher and farther than this one."

But Orville was wrong. Their large helicopter would not fly at all. "Why?" he asked. "It's just like the old one."

"Bigger," Wilbur reminded him.

"Then it should fly better," Orville said. "After all, a big buzzard flies better than a tiny robin."

Wilbur nodded to Orville and took the helicopter indoors. For two years it stood on a shelf in their room. Then on a fine spring day in 1881, Wilbur brought it down again.

10

"Why don't we try building another one?" he suggested.

"Let's get a kite instead," Orville said. "Everybody has one."

"Only *little* boys play with kites," Wilbur said. He was thirteen now and would soon be in high school.

"But we wouldn't be *playing*," said Orville. "We'd be experimenting. Maybe someday we'll know why that helicopter wouldn't fly."

"Well . . ." said Wilbur, and then he agreed.

The boys began saving their pennies. They did chores around the house to earn some extra money. When they had enough, they bought an orange-colored kite. It flew, but not well. "See how it dips and dives," said Orville.

"The wind must be pushing it," Wilbur explained. One day the wind pushed so hard the kite crashed into a tree.

"It will never fly again," Wilbur said, bringing it down. Orville looked disappointed. At supper that night they told what had happened.

"You boys could probably build your own kite," said Mrs. Wright. Neither of them had thought of that. They both started talking at once. They wanted to get to work right away.

"Wait a minute!" cried their father. "I have something else for you to do. We're going to move again. I'll need your help packing."

"Oh, dear!" Orville exclaimed. Even his mother seemed surprised.

"Back to Dayton?" Wilbur asked. He had lived in Dayton, Ohio, as a little boy, and Orville had been born there.

"No," said Bishop Wright. "This time we're going to Indiana. We'll live in a town called Richmond."

"Does it have plenty of wind?" asked Orville.

"I suppose so," said his father.

"Good," said Orville, smiling. "We can build our kite there."

Chapter *2*

The Kite Makers

Orville poked his head into the kitchen. "Aren't you through yet, Wil?" he asked.

"Almost," said Wilbur. There were only a few more dishes to wipe. He took out a dry towel, and in a moment the job was done.

He cleared the kitchen table and took some tissue paper and glue out of the cupboard. Orville brought in some old wooden crates. The boys were going to build their first kite. They would use wood for a framework.

"Draw it, *then* build it," Mrs. Wright said, coming into the kitchen. They looked at her, surprised.

"If it looks right on paper, it will be right when you make it," she said. She helped them draw the kite and then stood back, squinting her eyes.

"Maybe you'd better use wire *and* glue to hold the frame together," she said. "You want the kite to be strong."

Wilbur and Orville were speechless. Finally Wilbur said, "Mother, what do *you* know about making kites?"

16

"Nothing," she said, and her eyes twinkled. "But I know how to make things hold together. Look how long you've worn those overalls."

The boys took her advice. The kite they built was strong, and it flew beautifully. So they decided to build a bigger one. They got it into the air, but it crashed when the wind died down. What had they done wrong?

Suddenly Wilbur pointed to the sky. "Look at that hawk," he cried.

Orville looked up. "Watch him," said Wilbur. "There's hardly any wind, but he still stays up."

"His wings are curved," cried Orville.

"Yes," said Wilbur. "If we made a kite that curved in the wind, it might stay up too."

Their next kite had a thin frame that bent easily. In the wind it curved like a sail. The boys had been right. The kite flew higher and farther than any other one in the neighborhood.

A boy who lived nearby bought the kite. The brothers soon sold others. Wilbur and Orville spent nearly all their time building kites that summer. When fall came, school started. "Just when our business was doing so well," Orville sighed.

In Richmond, Wilbur and Orville went to different schools. Orville was ten and still in grade school. He loved doing arithmetic, but he hated homework. His teacher put him in the front row of the classroom to keep him out of mischief.

Wilbur was fourteen and in high school. He liked to play football and a game called "shinny." This was like ice hockey but played on land.

The boys still found time to work together. The old barn behind the house became their workshop. They learned to make a new kind of kite. It was shaped like a long box and had two wings fastened together. It was called a box kite.

The Wrights spent three years in Richmond. Then they moved back to Dayton. All of them were happy to see their old friends again.

Chapter 3

An Accident

Orville walked slowly up Hawthorne Street. Suddenly he saw the doctor's horse and wagon standing outside his house. He started to run. His mother met him at the door.

"It's Wilbur," she said. "He's had an accident."

21

Wilbur had been playing shinny, and a wooden club had hit him in the mouth. He had lost five teeth and a lot of blood. His mouth was so sore he could not eat. Three more teeth soon had to be pulled. The accident was a bad shock for Wilbur, and he was weak from lack of food.

At last Wilbur grew stronger. He would have to rest a long time and could not finish high school.

"Since you can't go back to school," Orville said one day, "I'll bring you books to read."

"Fine," Wilbur agreed. "I want everything you can find about flying." Men had tried to build flying machines for years. Not one machine had worked, but the inventors never stopped trying.

Lying in bed, Wilbur had plenty of time to think about flight, and to dream.

"Maybe you can find out why that big helicopter of ours wouldn't work," said Orville as he brought in a load of books. He was in eighth grade now. His best friend was Ed Sines, who lived down the street.

At Ed's house one day he saw a toy printing set. "Let's go into business," Orville said eagerly. "We could be partners."

The first thing they printed was a card that said, "Sines & Wright." Soon they were printing handbills for grocers to tell what foods were on sale.

Bishop Wright was very interested in the boys' work. "You're doing a fine job," he told them.

"We could do better if we had a real press," said Orville. A few days later Bishop Wright invited the boys out to the barn. There they saw a small hand press and a box of metal type.

"It's an old press, and it's not very big," said Bishop Wright. "But it is better than what you've got."

The press stayed in the barn, and the barn became the home of Sines & Wright. With the new equipment they could do more work. They decided to publish a newspaper for their eighth grade class.

They called it *The Midget*. It had four pages, but the boys had only enough stories for three. One page just had "Sines & Wright" printed on it twice.

"It seems that you boys got lazy," said Bishop Wright. "I don't think you should let anyone see this paper."

Orville was stunned. One hundred papers would be wasted. Later he was glad no one had read *The Midget*. One story had made fun of his teacher, who was very strict. It had said: *"Next week we propose to publish one of Miss Jennings' famous lectures before the pupils of The Intermediate School on the Inherent Wickedness of School Children."* Miss Jennings might have punished them for being so bold.

After that, Sines & Wright gave up the newspaper business and just did printing jobs for other people.

One day Orville came home from the print shop much earlier than usual.

Wilbur looked up from a magazine as Orville entered his room.

"Look at this," Wilbur cried. "A man in Germany can actually fly. He built a glider. It's a huge pair of wings that float on the wind. He runs downhill with the wings on, and they lift him."

"Why couldn't *we* do that?" Orville asked.

"Maybe we shall," said Wilbur. Then he looked hard at his brother. "Say, is anything wrong?"

Orville nodded and then explained. A customer had paid for a printing order with fresh popcorn on the cob instead of money. Orville wanted to sell the popcorn and buy parts for a new press. Ed wanted to keep the corn and eat it.

"Maybe we should just divide it," said Orville.

"Why not give him all of it?" Wilbur said.

"Why?" Orville asked, surprised.

"You could buy him out that way," Wilbur explained. "He'd have all the popcorn, but *you'd* have the printing business."

"But I'd still need a partner," said Orville. "I can't do everything alone."

"Can *I* apply for the job?" Wilbur asked. "The doctor says I'll be up and around soon."

"You're hired!" cried Orville. He was glad that the Wright brothers would be working together again.

Chapter *4*

The West Side News

Orville came into the house and flopped into a chair. "I think I've got enough material to build a new press," he told his brother. At the junkyard he had picked up pieces of wood, old wheels, an old iron roller and a grave-stone.

Orville could hardly wait to work as a printer all the time. He had only one more year of high school.

"I have the material, Wil," said Orville. "Now I need your help. Please make a design for the press."

"I'll start on it soon," his brother replied, "but I can't today. I promised Mother I'd read to her. She's staying in bed." Mrs. Wright had not been well for many months.

Wilbur helped Orville as much as he could. It was not easy to make a press out of junk, but they did.

Orville was happy when new printing jobs poured in. He decided to start another newspaper. It would be better than *The Midget*. He had learned a lot since then.

He rented a small room on West Third Street. In March, 1889, the first issue of *The West Side News* appeared.

It had stories and news about the people who lived on Dayton's west side. Orville needed more help in the shop, so Ed Sines came to work. He gathered news and sold ads.

Wilbur came to the shop too, as often as he could. He had to stay home a lot to care for Mrs. Wright. She was getting weaker and weaker. The whole family was worried about her illness. In the summer of 1889 she died.

Kate, who was still in high school, kept house now. She cooked for her father and for Wilbur and Orville. The older boys, Lorin and Reuchlin, had left home.

Wilbur was twenty-one and Orville seventeen. Both of them worked long hours. The print shop kept them busy.

One day a young man came into the shop. Instead of ordering some printing, he asked for some oil. Wilbur loaned him an oilcan, and the man went back outside.

Orville peeked through the window. "Look," he said. "He's using it to oil his bicycle."

"It's one of those new bikes," said Wilbur. "Both wheels are the same size, instead of one being bigger than the other."

The new design had come from Europe. It was very popular. Soon many people came to the print shop to borrow tools and fix their bicycles.

"You'd think we were repair men instead of printers," Wilbur said finally.

Orville looked up from the press.

"Why can't we be both?" he suggested. His brother and Ed Sines looked surprised. "More people are riding bikes every day," Orville went on. "The more bikes there are, the more work there'd be for us."

The brothers decided to let Ed Sines manage their printing business. In December, 1892, they rented a vacant store across the street from their print shop.

A few months later they watched as a sign was hung over their new door. The sign read, "Wright Cycle Shop."

Chapter 5

The Wright Flier

The floor of the Wright Cycle Shop was cluttered with bicycle parts. Orville wiped some grease from his arm. "If these bikes were better built, they wouldn't fall apart."

Wilbur only shrugged, but Orville went on. "*We* could build bicycles as good as these ourselves."

"Ours would be better!" said Wilbur.

"Of course," said Orville, firmly. The brothers looked at each other. Neither spoke, but it was already decided. They would make bikes as well as fix them.

The bikes were sturdily built. They rode well and needed few repairs. The only problem was getting people to buy them.

"Why don't I enter a bike race?" Orville said. "They're being held all the time now. If I do well, people will want to own bikes just like mine." Wilbur would have raced too, but he was still weak from his illness.

Orville practiced. He spent two hours every day riding his bike. On the day of the race, Wilbur went with him to the fairground. "Save your strength for the last few laps," he told Orville.

The racers lined up. The starter fired his pistol. The two-mile race began.

Orville was far behind at first. He let the others fight for the lead. Then slowly he caught up.

He was in fourth place at the end of the third lap. Then he pedaled harder. Soon he was third, then second. The sound of the crowd roared in his ears.

He was ahead now. The track was clear. He could see the finish line through the dust. Then *BANG!* The bike jumped. Its front tire had exploded. Orville fell to the ground, and the other bikes zoomed by. He had lost the race.

"It was our fault," said Wilbur. "We should have put on new tires. You've been riding on those old ones for a month."

"They looked all right," said Orville sadly. "I thought they would last."

Business at the bike shop was slow after that. Wilbur knew why. "People won't come to us if we can't keep our own bike in good repair," he said.

"The only thing to do is enter another race," said Orville.

The next week he took his bike to the fairground again. People laughed when he moved to the starting line. He did not even look up.

The starting signal was given, and Orville shot ahead. He pedaled with all his strength. He rolled across the finish line 100 yards in front of anyone else.

A man rushed up to him. "I'd like my son to have a bike like that," he exclaimed. "What do you call it?"

Orville was still out of breath, but he thought quickly. "Why, my brother and I call it . . . the *Wright Flier*," he said.

Business at the shop was good now. Many people bought the bicycles that Wilbur and Orville built. For several years the brothers worked hard making and selling bicycles.

Chapter *6*

Kites and Gliders

It was after midnight. A candle was burning low inside the shack behind the bicycle shop. Orville sat at a sewing machine. He was sewing pieces of white cloth together. Wilbur was finishing the frame of what looked like a big box kite.

It was five feet long. If it flew well, Wilbur and Orville would make a bigger one. It was the model for a glider.

Ever since Wilbur's illness they had been talking about flight and making plans. They had read books and articles. They had decided to build a glider they could fly in. Later they would try to make a flying machine.

The box kite was finished that night. The brothers were up again at dawn. They took their kite to a nearby hill.

Many young boys were there with their kites. They looked at the Wright brothers curiously. Wilbur was 32 and Orville was 28. His hair was thinning. They both looked too old to be playing with kites.

The brothers were too busy to see the people watching them. "We can't build a big glider until we know our design is right," said Wilbur.

A strong wind was needed to get a big glider into the air. Wind provided *lift*. When the wind died down, a glider had to be able to stay in the air.

"*We* must be the boss of our glider," warned Orville, "not the wind. No glider will be safe to fly in until we have complete control of it."

Their box kite worked fairly well. For better control they added a short, stubby wing to the front. This wing was called an *elevator*. It helped guide the kite up and down.

When they were ready to build a big glider, Wilbur said, "We won't be able to fly it in Dayton. We'll have to find a spot where the wind blows hard all the time." Flying would be safe only if the wind was steady.

Wilbur wrote to the United States
Weather Bureau in Washington, D. C.
Soon an answer came. "They suggest
a place on the coast of North Carolina."

"What's it called?" Orville asked.

Wilbur looked at the letter again to
be sure. Then he said, "Kitty Hawk."

Chapter *7*

Kitty Hawk

In September, 1900, the brothers were ready to go to Kitty Hawk. By this time Ed Sines had sold the printing business and was manager of the Wright Cycle Shop.

Kate Wright helped her brothers get ready. The glider had been taken apart and packed in big boxes. Wilbur left with the glider. Orville soon joined him.

Kitty Hawk had a wide, sandy beach that would be soft to land on. There was a weather station, a lifesaving station, and a post office.

The brothers camped in a tent on the beach. Orville cooked their meals on a gasoline stove. He even learned to make biscuits!

The beach was not very windy that month. The brothers searched and finally found a better spot about four miles away. It was called Kill Devil Hill, but it was really just a big sand dune.

Wilbur and Orville took turns flying. One of them would climb onto the lower wing of the glider and lie down. Then the other brother would start the glider down the side of the sand dune.

He would run along, holding one wing tip to balance the glider until the wind lifted it.

The first flights were not far off the ground. Wilbur and Orville did not care how high they went. They wanted to practice controlling their glider. It did not work well yet. It dipped and turned. Sometimes it hit the ground with a hard thump.

"We're not the boss of this glider," Orville said at last. "Maybe we'll do better with another model, next year."

Winter was coming. The wind off the sea was cold now. The brothers decided to go home. They planned to put tail fins on their new glider to help balance it in flight. They knew they had a lot of work ahead.

Chapter **8**

A Problem Is Solved

In July, 1901, the Wright brothers brought their second glider to Kitty Hawk. It was twice as big as the first one. "It should fly twice as well," said Orville.

He was wrong. This glider wobbled and shook. It could not be controlled at all in a strong wind.

"We still have a lot to learn," said Wilbur sadly. "We'd better go home."

Orville said, "The wings are the problem." He watched a sea gull glide over the beach. "Our glider should fly as smoothly as that bird. The wings just don't get enough lift."

At home the brothers decided to build a wind tunnel. They would test different wings in it, made of paper.

Their first wind tunnel was an old starch box with both ends open. A fan, driven by a gasoline motor, blew air through the tunnel.

The papers were fastened to what looked like a weather vane turned sideways. It spun slowly in the wind. Wilbur and Orville watched how the papers acted in different speeds of wind.

The brothers made more than one wind tunnel. They tested more than 200 different wing-shapes. Finally they knew why their big glider did not fly well.

It had been heavier as well as bigger than the small one. To fly well, it would have needed more than twice as much lift. Its wings should have been bigger and wider.

The brothers also figured out why their big helicopter had not flown. "Its power came from twisted rubber bands," Orville remembered. "They worked fine on the small model but were too weak for the big one."

"Our next glider will be better," said Wilbur, "now that we know what was wrong."

In August, 1902, the third glider was ready. The brothers took it apart, packed it, and left for Kitty Hawk. The wind was blowing angrily when they arrived.

"Our glider would crash in weather like this," said Wilbur. "We'll have to wait."

When the storm died down, they put the glider together and made a test flight. The glider steered poorly. No matter what the brothers did, they could not control it completely.

"The wind is still boss," said Orville. He was tired, but he could not sleep that night. He kept asking himself over and over, "What are we doing wrong?"

Finally he had an idea. He could hardly wait to tell Wilbur.

"Wil," he cried the next morning, "I think I've got it. It's the tail."

"The what?" Wilbur asked sleepily.

"The tail," said Orville. "If we could make the tail fins move, we might be able to steer better."

The tail of the glider had two fins. The brothers fixed them so they could be moved when pulled by wires.

Now the glider flew better. It needed only one thing to make it into a flying machine: *a motor*.

Chapter 9

Takeoff!

Loud popping sounds cut the quiet of night. "It's those Wright brothers," people said, awakened by the noise. Wilbur and Orville were building an airplane motor in the shack behind the bike shop.

People laughed at what the Wrights were trying to do. "Why do men as smart as those two waste time on such a silly invention?" they asked. Wilbur and Orville knew what people were saying, but they did not care.

In September, 1903, they took their flying machine and its motor to Kitty Hawk. The brothers looked as happy as little boys. It was hard to tell that Wilbur was 36 and Orville 32.

They put their airplane together, but the motor broke down on the very first turn. Two new parts were needed. The brothers sent the broken parts back to Dayton by express.

The new parts reached them on November 20. But bad weather had set in. The motor could not be tested until November 28. Then another part broke.

"We can't give up," Wilbur said. "We'll get a new part."

"We'd better not trust the express company this time," said Orville. "I'll go back to Dayton myself."

Orville did not return to Kitty Hawk until December 11. The next day the airplane was ready to fly. But there was not enough wind.

Hours passed as the brothers waited. They read. They talked. They walked around. "I told Father we might be back home by Christmas," said Orville unhappily. "I don't suppose we will."

On December 14 the brothers decided to try a flight, even though there was not much wind. They took their plane to Kill Devil Hill. They laid a narrow track in a straight line down the hill. Their airplane would slide along the track before taking off.

"I guess we both want to go first," said Wilbur. "Let's toss a coin." He flipped a silver dollar into the air.

"Heads," cried Orville.

"It's tails," said Wilbur. "I win."

They started the motor, and Wilbur stretched out on the lower wing. He pushed a small lever. The plane moved down the track.

It climbed a few feet. Then it stopped and dived into the sand. Wilbur was unhurt, but the plane was damaged. It could not be flown for three days.

The morning of December 17, 1903, was very cold. Clouds of sand blew over the frozen puddles on the beach. The wind was almost fierce. Flying would be dangerous, so once again the brothers waited.

An hour passed, then two and three. Finally they decided to go ahead. They could wait no longer.

"We won't need a hill," said Wilbur. "In this wind, we can take off right from the beach."

Four men and a boy came out to see the flight. They huddled together to keep warm as they watched the brothers put down the track.

"It's your turn now, Orv," said Wilbur. The two of them shook hands.

They started the motor, and Orville climbed aboard. He squinted to keep the blowing sand out of his eyes. He waved and pushed the lever. The plane began to move.

Wilbur ran along beside the track. After 40 feet the plane slowly raised itself.

One foot, two feet, and then it was over Wilbur's head. He stopped running.

Holding his breath, he watched the plane dip slightly. "Oh, no!" he cried hoarsely, but the plane shot up again.

In a moment it came down and landed gently. Orville climbed out, waving excitedly. "We've done it, Wil," he shouted. "It flew!"

The plane had been up only twelve seconds, but it had flown 120 feet. It was the first plane ever to fly under its own power.

At two o'clock that afternoon Wilbur and Orville walked to the weather station. They sent a telegram to their father. They told him they had each flown twice, and that their longest flight had lasted 59 seconds.

At the end of the message they said, "Home for Christmas."

Chapter *10*

Huffman Pasture

Kate opened the front door and gave a big smile. "Father," she called, "the boys are back."

Bishop Wright came slowly down the stairs to greet his sons. "You have given the world a fine new invention," he told them.

At that time, he was almost the only one who thought so. Newspapers printed little about the Wright brothers' flight.

Most editors did not believe it. "We'll show them," said Wilbur, hiding his disappointment. "We'll build a plane so good they'll *have* to take notice!"

By spring Wilbur and Orville had a new airplane. They needed a nice flat place to fly it. They got permission to use Huffman Pasture, near the railroad tracks just outside the town.

The new plane went higher and farther than the first one. People riding on the trains could watch the plane. But they still thought flying was a silly stunt. So did many scientists.

Soon the brothers were running out of money. They needed help so they could keep improving their plane.

Bishop Wright suggested that they write to the United States government.

"The Army might like to buy your invention," he told them. "It could be used for scouting an enemy."

The brothers wrote a letter, but the government said no. They decided to go to Europe. "Maybe we can get people in other countries interested in our work," Wilbur said hopefully.

A plane was crated and taken to France. There were long talks with the French government. But nothing came of them.

Wilbur and Orville returned to the United States. How happy they were when they heard from the Army again. This time the Signal Corps wanted to see how well the airplane flew. Some test flights were planned at Fort Meyer, Virginia.

But first the brothers took their new plane to Kitty Hawk. They wanted to make sure it worked properly. Now newspapermen came to watch them fly. The Wrights were becoming famous.

Later Orville took the plane to Fort Meyer. On September 3 he made his first flight. Hundreds of people were watching. He swooped over the field and waved. The crowd began to cheer.

The son of President Theodore Roosevelt was there. Later he told his father, *"The people went crazy. They could hardly believe their eyes."*

The government soon bought the design for the Wright brothers' plane. Now the people who had laughed at Wilbur and Orville were calling them heroes.

Meanwhile Wilbur had gone to France alone. The French government was interested in their plane now too. Wilbur uncrated the plane that had been brought to France earlier. In August he began flying it. The French people were thrilled. "Someday travelers may *fly* all over the world," people said.

Orville and Kate went to France to join Wilbur. A great many famous people came to see the Wright brothers fly, even the kings of England and Spain. French newspapers called Wilbur and Orville the "Kings of the Air."

When France bought the Wright design, Wilbur and Orville came home. They arrived in Dayton in May, 1909. Five weeks later, the city had a huge homecoming for them.

Early on the morning of June 17, every church bell and factory whistle went off at once. Then cannons boomed.

At ten o'clock a carriage came to get Wilbur and Orville. Their old friend Ed Sines was in it. He rode with them through the streets of Dayton. A parade was held in their honor. Later, fireworks lit up the night sky.

The next day two medals were given to Wilbur and Orville. One was from the state of Ohio. The other one came from the United States Congress.

That afternoon the brothers boarded a train for Washington, D. C. There they received two more medals. These were given to them by the President himself.

Chapter *11*

The Wright Company

The old sign saying "Wright Cycle Shop" had been taken down. A new sign had gone up. It read "The Wright Company." Wilbur and Orville were in the airplane business.

They built a factory in Dayton. Soon it was making two airplanes a month. Wilbur was head of the company.

He spent most of his time at his desk.

Orville was busy too, but he still did plenty of flying. He found time to open a flying school at Huffman Pasture.

"We can't sell airplanes to people who can't fly them," he said. Soon he had many students.

May 25, 1910, was an important day for Wilbur and Orville. They gave their father his first flight. Bishop Wright was 82, but he was not afraid. "Go higher!" he shouted. He had a fine time.

In 1912 Wilbur became ill. At first doctors did not think the illness was serious. Then they learned he had typhoid fever. Wilbur died on May 30. He was 45 years old. People all over the world were sad.

Though Orville was heartbroken, he kept on with his work. Now he was head of The Wright Company. He worked there for many years. He lived to be 76 years old.

One windy day when Orville was an old man, he watched some boys flying kites. He smiled, remembering the kites he and Wilbur had built when they were young. How far those kites had led them!

People had frowned at their big box-kite glider. People had even laughed at their flying machine. But that was long ago.

Since then airplanes had fought in two world wars. They had flown across every ocean and continent. They had explored the North and South Poles.

Planes now carried passengers, mail and cargo all over the world. Orville had lived to see it all happen. People could go where they wanted in hours instead of days.

As Orville watched the kites, he saw a plane flash by above them. He did not hear the sound of its engines until it had passed. It was flying faster than the speed of sound.

"Wilbur wouldn't have believed it," he said to himself. Then he laughed out loud. "And neither would I."